Recipe:

Rating: ☆☆☆☆☆ Difficulty: ☆☆☆☆☆ Prep Time: Cook Time:

Ingredients:

Cooking Instructions:

Thoughts and Notes:

Recipe:

Rating: ☆☆☆☆☆ Difficulty: ☆☆☆☆☆ Prep Time: _____ Cook Time: _____

Ingredients:

_____
_____
_____
_____
_____
_____

Cooking Instructions:

_____
_____
_____
_____
_____
_____
_____
_____
_____
_____

Thoughts and Notes:

_____
_____
_____
_____
_____

Recipe:

Rating: ☆☆☆☆☆ Difficulty: ☆☆☆☆☆ Prep Time: Cook Time:

Ingredients:

Cooking Instructions:

Thoughts and Notes:

Recipe:

Rating: ☆☆☆☆☆ Difficulty: ☆☆☆☆☆ Prep Time: Cook Time:

Ingredients:

_____
_____
_____
_____
_____
_____

Cooking Instructions:

_____
_____
_____
_____
_____
_____
_____
_____
_____
_____

Thoughts and Notes:

_____
_____
_____
_____
_____

Recipe:

Rating: ☆☆☆☆☆ Difficulty: ☆☆☆☆☆ Prep Time: Cook Time:

Ingredients:

Cooking Instructions:

Thoughts and Notes:

Recipe:

Rating: ☆☆☆☆☆ Difficulty: ☆☆☆☆☆ Prep Time: Cook Time:

Ingredients:

_____

_____

_____

_____

_____

_____

Cooking Instructions:

_____

_____

_____

_____

_____

_____

_____

_____

_____

_____

_____

Thoughts and Notes:

_____

_____

_____

_____

_____

Recipe:

Rating: ☆☆☆☆☆ Difficulty: ☆☆☆☆☆ Prep Time: Cook Time:

Ingredients:

Cooking Instructions:

Thoughts and Notes:

Recipe:

Rating: ☆☆☆☆☆ Difficulty: ☆☆☆☆☆ Prep Time: Cook Time:

Ingredients:

Cooking Instructions:

Thoughts and Notes:

Recipe:

Rating: ☆☆☆☆☆ Difficulty: ☆☆☆☆☆ Prep Time: Cook Time:

Ingredients:

Cooking Instructions:

Thoughts and Notes:

Recipe:

Rating: ☆☆☆☆☆ Difficulty: ☆☆☆☆☆ Prep Time: Cook Time:

Ingredients:

Cooking Instructions:

Thoughts and Notes:

Recipe:

Rating: ☆☆☆☆☆ Difficulty: ☆☆☆☆☆ Prep Time: Cook Time:

Ingredients:

Cooking Instructions:

Thoughts and Notes:

Recipe:

Rating: ☆☆☆☆☆ Difficulty: ☆☆☆☆☆ Prep Time: _____ Cook Time: _____

Ingredients:

_____
_____
_____
_____
_____
_____

Cooking Instructions:

_____
_____
_____
_____
_____
_____
_____
_____
_____
_____
_____

Thoughts and Notes:

_____
_____
_____
_____
_____

Recipe:

Rating: ☆☆☆☆☆ Difficulty: ☆☆☆☆☆ Prep Time: _____ Cook Time: _____

Ingredients:

Cooking Instructions:

Thoughts and Notes:

Recipe:

Rating: ☆☆☆☆☆ Difficulty: ✿✿✿✿✿ Prep Time: Cook Time:

Ingredients:

Cooking Instructions:

Thoughts and Notes:

Recipe:

Rating: ☆☆☆☆☆ Difficulty: ☆☆☆☆☆ Prep Time: Cook Time:

Ingredients:

Cooking Instructions:

Thoughts and Notes:

Recipe:

Rating: ☆☆☆☆☆ Difficulty: ☆☆☆☆☆ Prep Time: _____ Cook Time: _____

Ingredients:

_____

_____

_____

_____

_____

_____

Cooking Instructions:

_____

_____

_____

_____

_____

_____

_____

_____

_____

_____

_____

Thoughts and Notes:

_____

_____

_____

_____

_____

Recipe:

Rating: ☆☆☆☆☆ Difficulty: ☆☆☆☆☆ Prep Time: Cook Time:

Ingredients:

Cooking Instructions:

Thoughts and Notes:

Recipe:

Rating: ☆☆☆☆☆ Difficulty: ☆☆☆☆☆ Prep Time: _____ Cook Time: _____

Ingredients:
_____
_____
_____
_____
_____
_____

Cooking Instructions:
_____
_____
_____
_____
_____
_____
_____
_____
_____
_____
_____

Thoughts and Notes:
_____
_____
_____
_____
_____
_____

Recipe:

Rating: ☆☆☆☆☆ Difficulty: ☆☆☆☆☆ Prep Time: Cook Time:

Ingredients:

Cooking Instructions:

Thoughts and Notes:

Recipe:

Rating: ☆☆☆☆☆ Difficulty: ☆☆☆☆☆ Prep Time: Cook Time:

Ingredients:

Cooking Instructions:

Thoughts and Notes:

Recipe:

Rating: ☆☆☆☆☆ Difficulty: ☆☆☆☆☆ Prep Time: Cook Time:

Ingredients:

Cooking Instructions:

Thoughts and Notes:

Recipe:

Rating: ☆☆☆☆☆ Difficulty: ☆☆☆☆☆ Prep Time: Cook Time:

Ingredients:

_____

_____

_____

_____

_____

_____

Cooking Instructions:

_____

_____

_____

_____

_____

_____

_____

_____

_____

_____

_____

Thoughts and Notes:

_____

_____

_____

_____

_____

Recipe:

Rating: ☆☆☆☆☆ Difficulty: ☆☆☆☆☆ Prep Time: Cook Time:

Ingredients:

Cooking Instructions:

Thoughts and Notes:

Recipe:

Rating: ☆☆☆☆☆ Difficulty: ☆☆☆☆☆ Prep Time: _____ Cook Time: _____

Ingredients:

_____

_____

_____

_____

_____

_____

Cooking Instructions:

_____

_____

_____

_____

_____

_____

_____

_____

_____

_____

_____

_____

_____

Thoughts and Notes:

_____

_____

_____

_____

_____

_____

Recipe:

Rating: ☆☆☆☆☆ Difficulty: ☆☆☆☆☆ Prep Time: Cook Time:

Ingredients:

Cooking Instructions:

Thoughts and Notes:

Recipe:

Rating: ☆☆☆☆☆ Difficulty: ☆☆☆☆☆ Prep Time: Cook Time:

Ingredients:

_____
_____
_____
_____
_____
_____

Cooking Instructions:

_____
_____
_____
_____
_____
_____
_____
_____
_____
_____

Thoughts and Notes:

_____
_____
_____
_____
_____
_____

Recipe:

Rating: ☆☆☆☆☆ Difficulty: ☆☆☆☆☆ Prep Time: Cook Time:

Ingredients:

Cooking Instructions:

Thoughts and Notes:

Recipe:

Rating: ☆☆☆☆☆ Difficulty: ☆☆☆☆☆ Prep Time: Cook Time:

Ingredients:

Cooking Instructions:

Thoughts and Notes:

Recipe:

Rating: ☆☆☆☆☆ Difficulty: ☆☆☆☆☆ Prep Time: _____ Cook Time: _____

Ingredients:

_____

_____

_____

_____

_____

Cooking Instructions:

_____

_____

_____

_____

_____

_____

_____

_____

_____

Thoughts and Notes:

_____

_____

_____

_____

_____

Recipe:

Rating: ☆☆☆☆☆ Difficulty: ☆☆☆☆☆ Prep Time: Cook Time:

Ingredients:

Cooking Instructions:

Thoughts and Notes:

Recipe:

Rating: ☆☆☆☆☆ Difficulty: ☆☆☆☆☆ Prep Time: _____ Cook Time: _____

Ingredients:

_____

_____

_____

_____

_____

_____

Cooking Instructions:

_____

_____

_____

_____

_____

_____

_____

_____

_____

_____

_____

Thoughts and Notes:

_____

_____

_____

_____

_____

Recipe:

Rating: ☆☆☆☆☆ Difficulty: ☆☆☆☆☆ Prep Time: Cook Time:

Ingredients:

_____
_____
_____
_____
_____
_____

Cooking Instructions:

_____
_____
_____
_____
_____
_____
_____
_____
_____
_____

Thoughts and Notes:

_____
_____
_____
_____
_____
_____

Recipe:

Rating: ☆☆☆☆☆ Difficulty: ☆☆☆☆☆ Prep Time: Cook Time:

Ingredients:

Cooking Instructions:

Thoughts and Notes:

Recipe:

Rating: ☆☆☆☆☆ Difficulty: ✿✿✿✿✿ Prep Time: _____ Cook Time: _____

Ingredients:
_____
_____
_____
_____
_____
_____

Cooking Instructions:
_____
_____
_____
_____
_____
_____
_____
_____
_____
_____
_____

Thoughts and Notes:
_____
_____
_____
_____
_____

Recipe:

Rating: ☆☆☆☆☆ Difficulty: ☆☆☆☆☆ Prep Time: Cook Time:

Ingredients:

Cooking Instructions:

Thoughts and Notes:

Recipe:

Rating: ☆☆☆☆☆ Difficulty: ☆☆☆☆☆ Prep Time: Cook Time:

Ingredients:

Cooking Instructions:

Thoughts and Notes:

Recipe:

Rating: ☆☆☆☆☆ Difficulty: ☆☆☆☆☆ Prep Time: Cook Time:

Ingredients:

Cooking Instructions:

Thoughts and Notes:

Recipe:

Rating: ☆☆☆☆☆ Difficulty: ☆☆☆☆☆ Prep Time: Cook Time:

Ingredients:

Cooking Instructions:

Thoughts and Notes:

Recipe:

Rating: ☆☆☆☆☆ Difficulty: ☆☆☆☆☆ Prep Time: Cook Time:

Ingredients:

Cooking Instructions:

Thoughts and Notes:

Recipe:

Rating: ☆☆☆☆☆ Difficulty: ☆☆☆☆☆ Prep Time: _____ Cook Time: _____

Ingredients:
_____
_____
_____
_____
_____
_____

Cooking Instructions:
_____
_____
_____
_____
_____
_____
_____
_____
_____
_____
_____

Thoughts and Notes:
_____
_____
_____
_____
_____
_____

Recipe:

Rating: ☆☆☆☆☆ Difficulty: ☆☆☆☆☆ Prep Time: _____ Cook Time: _____

Ingredients:

_____

_____

_____

_____

_____

_____

Cooking Instructions:

_____

_____

_____

_____

_____

_____

_____

_____

_____

_____

_____

Thoughts and Notes:

_____

_____

_____

_____

_____

Recipe:

Rating: ☆☆☆☆☆ Difficulty: ☆☆☆☆☆ Prep Time: _____ Cook Time: _____

Ingredients:
_____
_____
_____
_____
_____
_____
_____

Cooking Instructions:
_____
_____
_____
_____
_____
_____
_____
_____
_____
_____
_____
_____
_____

Thoughts and Notes:
_____
_____
_____
_____
_____
_____

Recipe:

Rating: ☆☆☆☆☆ Difficulty: ☆☆☆☆☆ Prep Time: Cook Time:

Ingredients:

Cooking Instructions:

Thoughts and Notes:

Recipe:

Rating: ☆☆☆☆☆ Difficulty: ☆☆☆☆☆ Prep Time: Cook Time:

Ingredients:

_____

_____

_____

_____

_____

_____

Cooking Instructions:

_____

_____

_____

_____

_____

_____

_____

_____

_____

_____

Thoughts and Notes:

_____

_____

_____

_____

_____

_____

Recipe:

Rating: ☆☆☆☆☆ Difficulty: ☆☆☆☆☆ Prep Time: Cook Time:

Ingredients:

Cooking Instructions:

Thoughts and Notes:

Recipe:

Rating: ☆☆☆☆☆ Difficulty: ☆☆☆☆☆ Prep Time: Cook Time:

Ingredients:

Cooking Instructions:

Thoughts and Notes:

Recipe:

Rating: ☆☆☆☆☆ Difficulty: ☆☆☆☆☆ Prep Time: Cook Time:

Ingredients:

Cooking Instructions:

Thoughts and Notes:

Recipe:

Rating: ☆☆☆☆☆ Difficulty: ☆☆☆☆☆ Prep Time: Cook Time:

Ingredients:

_____

_____

_____

_____

_____

_____

Cooking Instructions:

_____

_____

_____

_____

_____

_____

_____

_____

_____

_____

_____

Thoughts and Notes:

_____

_____

_____

_____

_____

Recipe:

Rating: ☆☆☆☆☆ Difficulty: ☆☆☆☆☆ Prep Time: Cook Time:

Ingredients:

Cooking Instructions:

Thoughts and Notes:

Recipe:

Rating: ☆☆☆☆☆ Difficulty: ☆☆☆☆☆ Prep Time: Cook Time:

Ingredients:

Cooking Instructions:

Thoughts and Notes:

Recipe:

Rating: ☆☆☆☆☆ Difficulty: ☆☆☆☆☆ Prep Time: Cook Time:

Ingredients:

Cooking Instructions:

Thoughts and Notes:

Recipe:

Rating: ☆☆☆☆☆ Difficulty: ☆☆☆☆☆ Prep Time: Cook Time:

Ingredients:

Cooking Instructions:

Thoughts and Notes:

Recipe:

Rating: ☆☆☆☆☆ Difficulty: ☆☆☆☆☆ Prep Time: Cook Time:

Ingredients:

Cooking Instructions:

Thoughts and Notes:

Recipe:

Rating: ☆☆☆☆☆ Difficulty: ✿✿✿✿✿ Prep Time: Cook Time:

Ingredients:

Cooking Instructions:

Thoughts and Notes:

Recipe:

Rating: ☆☆☆☆☆ Difficulty: ☆☆☆☆☆ Prep Time: Cook Time:

Ingredients:

Cooking Instructions:

Thoughts and Notes:

Recipe:

Rating: ☆☆☆☆☆ Difficulty: ☆☆☆☆☆ Prep Time: _____ Cook Time: _____

Ingredients:

_____

_____

_____

_____

_____

_____

_____

Cooking Instructions:

_____

_____

_____

_____

_____

_____

_____

_____

_____

_____

_____

Thoughts and Notes:

_____

_____

_____

_____

_____

_____

Recipe:

Rating: ☆☆☆☆☆ Difficulty: ☆☆☆☆☆ Prep Time: Cook Time:

Ingredients:

Cooking Instructions:

Thoughts and Notes:

Recipe:

Rating: ☆☆☆☆☆ Difficulty: ☆☆☆☆☆ Prep Time: Cook Time:

Ingredients:

_____

_____

_____

_____

_____

_____

Cooking Instructions:

_____

_____

_____

_____

_____

_____

_____

_____

_____

_____

Thoughts and Notes:

_____

_____

_____

_____

_____

Recipe:

Rating: ☆☆☆☆☆ Difficulty: ☆☆☆☆☆ Prep Time: Cook Time:

Ingredients:

Cooking Instructions:

Thoughts and Notes:

Recipe:

Rating: ☆☆☆☆☆ Difficulty: ☆☆☆☆☆ Prep Time: _____ Cook Time:

Ingredients:

_____
_____
_____
_____
_____
_____

Cooking Instructions:

_____
_____
_____
_____
_____
_____
_____
_____
_____
_____
_____

Thoughts and Notes:

_____
_____
_____
_____
_____

Recipe:

Rating: ☆☆☆☆☆ Difficulty: ☆☆☆☆☆ Prep Time: Cook Time:

Ingredients:

Cooking Instructions:

Thoughts and Notes:

Recipe:

Rating: ☆☆☆☆☆ Difficulty: ☆☆☆☆☆ Prep Time: Cook Time:

Ingredients:

Cooking Instructions:

Thoughts and Notes:

Recipe:

Rating: ☆☆☆☆☆ Difficulty: ☆☆☆☆☆ Prep Time: Cook Time:

Ingredients:

Cooking Instructions:

Thoughts and Notes:

Recipe:

Rating: ☆☆☆☆☆ Difficulty: ☆☆☆☆☆ Prep Time: Cook Time:

Ingredients:

_____

_____

_____

_____

_____

_____

Cooking Instructions:

_____

_____

_____

_____

_____

_____

_____

_____

_____

_____

_____

Thoughts and Notes:

_____

_____

_____

_____

_____

Recipe:

Rating: ☆☆☆☆☆ Difficulty: ☆☆☆☆☆ Prep Time: Cook Time:

Ingredients:

Cooking Instructions:

Thoughts and Notes:

Recipe:

Rating: ☆☆☆☆☆ Difficulty: ☆☆☆☆☆ Prep Time: _____ Cook Time: _____

Ingredients:
_____
_____
_____
_____
_____
_____

Cooking Instructions:
_____
_____
_____
_____
_____
_____
_____
_____
_____
_____
_____

Thoughts and Notes:
_____
_____
_____
_____
_____

Recipe:

Rating: ☆☆☆☆☆ Difficulty: ☆☆☆☆☆ Prep Time:　　　　　Cook Time:

Ingredients:

Cooking Instructions:

Thoughts and Notes:

Recipe:

Rating: ☆☆☆☆☆ Difficulty: ☆☆☆☆☆ Prep Time: Cook Time:

Ingredients:

Cooking Instructions:

Thoughts and Notes:

Recipe:

Rating: ☆☆☆☆☆ Difficulty: ☆☆☆☆☆ Prep Time: Cook Time:

Ingredients:

Cooking Instructions:

Thoughts and Notes:

Recipe:

Rating: ☆☆☆☆☆ Difficulty: ☆☆☆☆☆ Prep Time: Cook Time:

Ingredients:

Cooking Instructions:

Thoughts and Notes:

Recipe:

Rating: ☆☆☆☆☆ Difficulty: ☆☆☆☆☆ Prep Time: Cook Time:

Ingredients:

Cooking Instructions:

Thoughts and Notes:

Recipe:

Rating: ☆☆☆☆☆ Difficulty: ☆☆☆☆☆ Prep Time: Cook Time:

Ingredients:

Cooking Instructions:

Thoughts and Notes:

Recipe:

Rating: ☆☆☆☆☆ Difficulty: ☆☆☆☆☆ Prep Time: Cook Time:

Ingredients:

Cooking Instructions:

Thoughts and Notes:

Recipe:

Rating: ☆☆☆☆☆ Difficulty: ✿✿✿✿✿ Prep Time: Cook Time:

Ingredients:

Cooking Instructions:

Thoughts and Notes:

Recipe:

Rating: ☆☆☆☆☆ Difficulty: ☆☆☆☆☆ Prep Time: Cook Time:

Ingredients:

Cooking Instructions:

Thoughts and Notes:

Recipe:

Rating: ☆☆☆☆☆ Difficulty: ☆☆☆☆☆ Prep Time: Cook Time:

Ingredients:

Cooking Instructions:

Thoughts and Notes:

Recipe:

Rating: ☆☆☆☆☆ Difficulty: ☆☆☆☆☆ Prep Time: Cook Time:

Ingredients:

Cooking Instructions:

Thoughts and Notes:

Recipe:

Rating: ☆☆☆☆☆ Difficulty: ☆☆☆☆☆ Prep Time: Cook Time:

Ingredients:

Cooking Instructions:

Thoughts and Notes:

Recipe:

Rating: ☆☆☆☆☆ Difficulty: ☆☆☆☆☆ Prep Time: Cook Time:

Ingredients:

Cooking Instructions:

Thoughts and Notes:

Recipe:

Rating: ☆☆☆☆☆ Difficulty: ☆☆☆☆☆ Prep Time: Cook Time:

Ingredients:

Cooking Instructions:

Thoughts and Notes:

Recipe:

Rating: ☆☆☆☆☆ Difficulty: ☆☆☆☆☆ Prep Time:　　　　　　Cook Time:

Ingredients:

Cooking Instructions:

Thoughts and Notes:

Recipe:

Rating: ☆☆☆☆☆ Difficulty: ☆☆☆☆☆ Prep Time: Cook Time:

Ingredients:
_____
_____
_____
_____
_____
_____

Cooking Instructions:
_____
_____
_____
_____
_____
_____
_____
_____
_____
_____
_____

Thoughts and Notes:
_____
_____
_____
_____
_____
_____

Recipe:

Rating: ☆☆☆☆☆ Difficulty: ☆☆☆☆☆ Prep Time: Cook Time:

Ingredients:

Cooking Instructions:

Thoughts and Notes:

Recipe:

Rating: ☆☆☆☆☆ Difficulty: ☆☆☆☆☆ Prep Time: Cook Time:

Ingredients:

Cooking Instructions:

Thoughts and Notes:

Recipe:

Rating: ☆☆☆☆☆ Difficulty: ☆☆☆☆☆ Prep Time: Cook Time:

Ingredients:

Cooking Instructions:

Thoughts and Notes:

Recipe:

Rating: ☆☆☆☆☆ Difficulty: ☆☆☆☆☆ Prep Time: _____ Cook Time: _____

Ingredients: _____

_____

_____

_____

_____

_____

_____

Cooking Instructions: _____

_____

_____

_____

_____

_____

_____

_____

_____

_____

_____

_____

_____

Thoughts and Notes: _____

_____

_____

_____

_____

_____

Recipe:

Rating: ☆☆☆☆☆ Difficulty: ☆☆☆☆☆ Prep Time: Cook Time:

Ingredients:

Cooking Instructions:

Thoughts and Notes:

Recipe:

Rating: ☆☆☆☆☆ Difficulty: ☆☆☆☆☆ Prep Time: Cook Time:

Ingredients:

Cooking Instructions:

Thoughts and Notes:

Recipe:

Rating: ☆☆☆☆☆ Difficulty: ☆☆☆☆☆ Prep Time: Cook Time:

Ingredients:

Cooking Instructions:

Thoughts and Notes:

Recipe:

Rating: ☆☆☆☆☆ Difficulty: ☆☆☆☆☆ Prep Time: Cook Time:

Ingredients:

Cooking Instructions:

Thoughts and Notes:

Recipe:

Rating: ☆☆☆☆☆ Difficulty: ☆☆☆☆☆ Prep Time: Cook Time:

Ingredients:

Cooking Instructions:

Thoughts and Notes:

Recipe:

Rating: ☆☆☆☆☆ Difficulty: ☆☆☆☆☆ Prep Time: Cook Time:

Ingredients:

_____
_____
_____
_____
_____
_____

Cooking Instructions:

_____
_____
_____
_____
_____
_____
_____
_____
_____
_____
_____

Thoughts and Notes:

_____
_____
_____
_____
_____

Recipe:

Rating: ☆☆☆☆☆ Difficulty: ☆☆☆☆☆ Prep Time: Cook Time:

Ingredients:

Cooking Instructions:

Thoughts and Notes:

Recipe:

Rating: ☆☆☆☆☆ Difficulty: ☆☆☆☆☆ Prep Time: Cook Time:

Ingredients:

Cooking Instructions:

Thoughts and Notes:

Recipe:

Rating: ☆☆☆☆☆ Difficulty: ☆☆☆☆☆ Prep Time: Cook Time:

Ingredients:

Cooking Instructions:

Thoughts and Notes:

Recipe:

Rating: ☆☆☆☆☆ Difficulty: ☆☆☆☆☆ Prep Time: Cook Time:

Ingredients:

Cooking Instructions:

Thoughts and Notes:

Recipe:

Rating: ☆☆☆☆☆ Difficulty: ☆☆☆☆☆ Prep Time: Cook Time:

Ingredients:

Cooking Instructions:

Thoughts and Notes:

Recipe:

Rating: ☆☆☆☆☆ Difficulty: ☆☆☆☆☆ Prep Time: Cook Time:

Ingredients:

Cooking Instructions:

Thoughts and Notes:

Recipe:

Rating: ☆☆☆☆☆ Difficulty: ☆☆☆☆☆ Prep Time: Cook Time:

Ingredients:

Cooking Instructions:

Thoughts and Notes:

Recipe:

Rating: ☆☆☆☆☆ Difficulty: ☆☆☆☆☆ Prep Time: Cook Time:

Ingredients:

_____

_____

_____

_____

_____

_____

Cooking Instructions:

_____

_____

_____

_____

_____

_____

_____

_____

_____

_____

_____

Thoughts and Notes:

_____

_____

_____

_____

_____

Recipe:

Rating: ☆☆☆☆☆ Difficulty: ☆☆☆☆☆ Prep Time: Cook Time:

Ingredients:

Cooking Instructions:

Thoughts and Notes:

Recipe:

Rating: ☆☆☆☆☆ Difficulty: ☆☆☆☆☆ Prep Time: Cook Time:

Ingredients:

Cooking Instructions:

Thoughts and Notes:

Recipe:

Rating: ☆☆☆☆☆ Difficulty: ☆☆☆☆☆ Prep Time: Cook Time:

Ingredients:

Cooking Instructions:

Thoughts and Notes:

Recipe:

Rating: ☆☆☆☆☆ Difficulty: ☆☆☆☆☆ Prep Time: _____ Cook Time: _____

Ingredients:

_____

_____

_____

_____

_____

_____

Cooking Instructions:

_____

_____

_____

_____

_____

_____

_____

_____

_____

_____

_____

Thoughts and Notes:

_____

_____

_____

_____

_____

Recipe:

Rating: ☆☆☆☆☆ Difficulty: ☆☆☆☆☆ Prep Time: Cook Time:

Ingredients:

Cooking Instructions:

Thoughts and Notes:

Recipe:

Rating: ☆☆☆☆☆ Difficulty: ☆☆☆☆☆ Prep Time: Cook Time:

Ingredients:

Cooking Instructions:

Thoughts and Notes:

Recipe:

Rating: ☆☆☆☆☆ Difficulty: ☆☆☆☆☆ Prep Time: Cook Time:

Ingredients:

Cooking Instructions:

Thoughts and Notes:

Recipe:

Rating: ☆☆☆☆☆ Difficulty: ☆☆☆☆☆ Prep Time: Cook Time:

Ingredients:

Cooking Instructions:

Thoughts and Notes:

Recipe:

Rating: ☆☆☆☆☆ Difficulty: ☆☆☆☆☆ Prep Time: Cook Time:

Ingredients:

Cooking Instructions:

Thoughts and Notes:

Recipe:

Rating: ☆☆☆☆☆ Difficulty: ☆☆☆☆☆ Prep Time: Cook Time:

Ingredients:

_____

_____

_____

_____

_____

_____

Cooking Instructions:

_____

_____

_____

_____

_____

_____

_____

_____

_____

_____

_____

Thoughts and Notes:

_____

_____

_____

_____

_____

_____

Recipe:

Rating: ☆☆☆☆☆ Difficulty: ☆☆☆☆☆ Prep Time: Cook Time:

Ingredients:

Cooking Instructions:

Thoughts and Notes:

Recipe:

Rating: ☆☆☆☆☆ Difficulty: ☆☆☆☆☆ Prep Time: _____ Cook Time: _____

Ingredients:

_____
_____
_____
_____
_____
_____
_____

Cooking Instructions:

_____
_____
_____
_____
_____
_____
_____
_____
_____
_____
_____
_____
_____

Thoughts and Notes:

_____
_____
_____
_____
_____
_____
_____

Recipe:

Rating: ☆☆☆☆☆ Difficulty: ☆☆☆☆☆ Prep Time: Cook Time:

Ingredients:

Cooking Instructions:

Thoughts and Notes:

Recipe:

Rating: ☆☆☆☆☆ Difficulty: ☆☆☆☆☆ Prep Time: Cook Time:

Ingredients:

Cooking Instructions:

Thoughts and Notes:

Recipe:

Rating: ☆☆☆☆☆ Difficulty: ☆☆☆☆☆ Prep Time: Cook Time:

Ingredients:

Cooking Instructions:

Thoughts and Notes:

Recipe:

Rating: ☆☆☆☆☆ Difficulty: ☆☆☆☆☆ Prep Time: Cook Time:

Ingredients:

_____

_____

_____

_____

_____

_____

Cooking Instructions:

_____

_____

_____

_____

_____

_____

_____

_____

_____

_____

_____

Thoughts and Notes:

_____

_____

_____

_____

_____

_____

Recipe:

Rating: ☆☆☆☆☆ Difficulty: ☆☆☆☆☆ Prep Time: Cook Time:

Ingredients:

Cooking Instructions:

Thoughts and Notes:

Recipe:

Rating: ☆☆☆☆☆ Difficulty: ☆☆☆☆☆ Prep Time: Cook Time:

Ingredients:

_____

_____

_____

_____

_____

Cooking Instructions:

_____

_____

_____

_____

_____

_____

_____

_____

_____

_____

_____

Thoughts and Notes:

_____

_____

_____

_____

_____

Recipe:

Rating: ☆☆☆☆☆ Difficulty: ☆☆☆☆☆ Prep Time: Cook Time:

Ingredients:

Cooking Instructions:

Thoughts and Notes:

Recipe:

Rating: ☆☆☆☆☆ Difficulty: ☆☆☆☆☆ Prep Time: Cook Time:

Ingredients:

Cooking Instructions:

Thoughts and Notes:

Printed in the USA
CPSIA information can be obtained
at www.ICGtesting.com
LVHW012218181223
766859LV00012B/704